meditation

express

STRESS
RELIEF
IN
60 SECONDS
FLAT

Nancy L. Butler-Ross and Michael Suib

CONTEMPORARY BOOKS

Library of Congress Cataloging-in-Publication Data

Butler-Ross, Nancy.
    Meditation express / Nancy L. Butler-Ross and Michael Suib.
       p.   cm.
    Includes bibliographical references and index.
    ISBN 0-8092-9774-4
    1. Meditation.   I. Suib, Michael.   II. Title.
  BF637.M4B88   2001
  158.1'2—dc21   00-34636
                                                CIP

We are grateful to the following people (and their assistants) for granting
us kind permission to use their words and thoughts as part of this book:
    Ram Dass quotation is used with the permission of Ram Dass.
    Rita Rudner quotation is used with the permission of Rita Rudner.
    Jane Wagner quotations are used with the permission of Jane Wagner.
    Quotation from *The Appointments of Dennis Jennings* is used with the
permission of Steven Wright.
    Gilda Radner quotation is used with the permission of Michael F. Radner.
    The F.A.S.T. Hand Chart is used with the permission of David Burmeister,
Director, Jin Shin Jyutsu, Inc.

Meditation is an effective way to manage stress. However, the meditations in
this book are not medical prescriptions nor are they meant to be used in lieu
of medical treatment.

Cover and interior design by Monica Baziuk

Published by Contemporary Books
A division of NTC/Contemporary Publishing Group, Inc.
4255 West Touhy Avenue, Lincolnwood (Chicago), Illinois 60712-1975 U.S.A.
Printed in the United States of America
International Standard Book Number: 0-8092-9774-4
01 02 03 04 05 06 LB 15 14 13 12 11 10 9 8 7 6 5 4 3 2 1

Contents

Acknowledgments

As novice-as-they-come, fledgling writer-wannabes, we offer our deepest gratitude to:

Jeff Rutherford, who first saw the possibilities in our idea of a book of quick and easy meditations.

Our agent, Denise Marcil, and her staff for their ability to deal with not just one but two neophyte authors. Their tremendous amount of hand-holding, patience, and encouragement earned our respect, applause, and thanks.

NTC/Contemporary Publishing for having enough faith in *Meditation Express* and us as first-time authors to publish this book.

Judith McCarthy, our editor, for her enthusiasm and gentle manner in guiding us through the difficult transition from manuscript to bookstore shelf.

All of the agents and publishers who compassionately rejected our book proposal with constructive criticism.

We would like to thank our many friends whose love and support helped us to conceive and birth this book, particularly:

Ann Evonich Wyncoop, who taught us the basics of centering, meditation, healing, and trust.

Doug Grunther of WDST-FM radio, an old friend who didn't blink at the idea of doing meditation on his show, *The Woodstock Round Table*; his producer, Elda Stiletto, who pared the meditations down to byte-size pieces; and the early rising knights: Studio Stu, Gus Mancini, Owen Swenson, Martha Frankel, Simone Felice, The Hawk Project, and Shadow. Thanks for your many forms of backup.

The Woodstock Sunday Poetry & Potluck Salon: Lew and Sandy Gardner, Cynthia and Peter Kudren,

Beatrice Videz, Tara Johannsen, and Ilfra Haley, for being our initial cheerleaders.

Our dear friends who acted as mentors, muses, sanity suppliers, editors, and devil's advocates: Roberta Wilson and Frank Mendelson, Nancy Thomassian, Nancy Wyncoop-Bower, Tom Hatlestad, Peg Dukas, Maria DuBois, Samata Horowitz, Abigail Robin, Toni Ann Mazza, the staff and friends at the Woodstock Library, and The Gypsy Wolf Cantina, who helped to feed our bodies and souls. The Key West Poetry Guild; the Key West Library staff; Deborah and Sheldon Mermelstein; Karen Harte; Jane Phillips; Jo Ann Lordahl; Annie and Nikki Mermelstein; Bill Meredith; Dana Clark and Michael McClure; Beanie, Blair, and Gizmo Einstein; Doug Bryan; Linda Baxter and Michael Connelly; Celine and Alex Ezpeleta and Michael Haskins; Tim Behan; Karin Rainbow and Eddie Matthis; Sicily Nick; Dee and John Boles; Liz McClelland and Michael Durkas. Sailors extraordinaire George Claing, Capt. Dave Samson and Charlie-mon, and all of our extended family at Marlin Pier and the Garrison Bight Marina.

Special thanks to people without whom none of this would have been possible:

Herb and Judy Suib, who played matchmakers.

Mom and Bill Gunther, who proved that you're never too old to fall in love and live happily ever after.

Mom and Pop, true soul mates to the end.

Takk

Gracias

Salamat

Thank you!

A Note from Nancy

For years I have been teaching meditation classes to businesspeople, nurses, housewives, and college students who wanted to find a sense of inner serenity and balance in their lives. My classes were always popular and well attended, with participants enjoying the concepts of meditation and deriving some of its health benefits.

But I found that very few people continued to meditate between classes; their most frequent excuses were:

- I can't take the time.

- People think I'm weird if I just sit around with my eyes closed.

- There's no place in the house or dorm that's quiet.

My life partner, husband, and coauthor, Michael Suib, who has had years of experience with centering, hypnotherapy, and energy balancing, also had his own problems and excuses for not meditating. His favorite dodge for not meditating was, "My mind keeps wandering so fuhggedabowdit."

As with all great inspirations, the concept of combining the seeming opposites of "quick" and "meditation" slowly broke like the perfect dawn.

Together, Michael and I developed a series of one- to two-minute meditations that could be done anywhere: in the shower, walking up the stairs, or while on hold on the telephone. We tried to demystify the process and gave the meditations a present-day tone. We worked to make the meditations easy to do and to clarify the concept that the *act* of meditating for *any* length of time is beneficial in itself; there's no pressure to reach enlightenment or meditate "perfectly."

I introduced my students to the concept of meditation as a way to **wake up** their abilities to keep their thoughts focused in the present moment and not to be distracted by the mild chaos usually surrounding them. You will find this is a recurring theme throughout the entire book.

As I used this new approach in my classes, my students started to call me, excited about how they'd meditated between meetings and classes and used our meditations to help them stay alert, deal with difficult supervisors, and keep a sense of balance and perspective in their lives. We joked that these meditations were like one-minute prescriptions, or an *Mx*, for stress relief, which is how they're presented in this book.

Buoyed by this success, I approached a friend who is the host of a long-running, successful radio talk program and declared that I wanted to offer guided meditations on his show. He loved the idea and enthusiastically promoted me, dubbing me WDST-FM's "Official Radio Meditator." That was in April 1996; since then I've been a guest on his show every week, and the audience response has been enthusiastic. It seems as though everyone is now meditating, from senior citizens to single moms to insurance executives.

Michael and I sincerely believe that *anyone* can meditate. If you've meditated in the past but stopped because you no longer have the time, or if you've been put off by the mysticism and mystique that often surround meditation, we're sure you'll enjoy our simple and easy approach. Enjoy.

—*Nancy L. Butler-Ross*

Introduction

Meditation is easy, effortless, exhilarating!

Got a minute?

Meditation Express is a method to help you get on the right track toward making your complete mind-body-soul connections and a way to train yourself to be in touch with your peaceful, all-knowing inner center of balance throughout your day. *Anyone can meditate.*

Many of us know that a few moments of connecting with our inner resources can have dramatic and healthy effects in restoring a sense of balance to a hectic day. But who has the luxury of spending 45 minutes to one hour calming themselves down in the middle of a rushed day? (Hooray for you if you do. We encourage you to meditate for as long as you can, and be sure to browse Appendix C for a list of books with longer meditations.) The meditations in *Meditation Express* are designed to be done in one to two minutes (no, that's not a typo). The point is not how long you meditate but to meditate!

We each meditate differently and for different reasons. Nancy meditates to be in touch with all parts of herself—the many facets of being human, with a heart *and* a mind—and also to be in touch with the part of herself that is unlimited, that has deep wisdom and is a source of renewal and guidance—her center.

Michael meditates not to find his inner self but to step back and take a moment to find a balance so that he can prevent an inner explosion that is not good for his family, friends, business associates, and least of all for himself.

Whatever *your* reasons are for meditating—whether your life is filled with high tension and pressures from business, family, and life in general or you have a sense of something missing in your life—or both—the exercises and meditations in this book will work for you.

These meditations are for everyone: experienced meditators, new meditators, and nonmeditators. If you've ever daydreamed or "spaced out" in line at the grocery store checkout counter, you can meditate.

These exercises are simple, easy, and filled with fun ideas to help you stay in touch with your own center. They encompass mindfulness, creative visualization, relaxation, and pure bliss. There's no right or wrong way to meditate.

The hardest part of meditating is to remember to do it!

The goals of *Meditation Express* are to:

- Calm your mind.

- Relax your body.

- Give you a quick and easy tool for stress reduction.

Meditation is not a religion. Webster's definition of meditation is from the Latin "meditare," meaning to reflect on, to ponder, to plan or intend in the mind, to engage in contemplation. You don't have to change your lifestyle or beliefs to do these meditations. We hope you'll make them a part of your everyday lifestyle, whether you wear blue jeans or Brooks Brothers suits. Our intent is to make these meditations so simple and easy to do that you'll want to do them every day. We also encourage you to do them whenever and wherever (in the elevator or in the shower) you can. Flexibility, comfort, and adaptability are our key words—you don't need a temple or a time clock to benefit from these meditations.

Michael is usually up and in the thick of his day before he stops to meditate. Nancy, on the other hand, won't leave her bed before meditating.

Michael meditates as a way to "fix" stress. For example, he'll meditate if he feels like he's going to scream at the kids or if worry and angst have projected him so far into the future that he can't think clearly about the here and now.

Nancy meditates as a preventive measure. For example, she'll meditate a few minutes throughout the day to "re-member" herself and reconnect with her wholeness and to spend a few moments feeling an inner serenity and calmness. It enables her to feel a strong sense of her direction and helps her to keep her perspective and sense of joy throughout the day.

Obviously, we use different approaches to meditation, but the end result is the same: a sense of harmony where we live in the present moment and balance for our bodies, minds, spirits, and emotions.

We also find it interesting that even though we have different approaches, we can both benefit from the same meditation exercises. Amazingly, we are also able to work together to create wonderful meditations.

Whatever *your* approach is to meditating, you can do these exercises anyplace, anytime: at home; at work; on the train, subway, or bus. But, Nancy also reminds her listeners, *never* meditate when you're driving, operating heavy machinery, or performing brain surgery.

The Benefits from Meditating

The benefits from meditation are individual and many. Nancy uses meditation to **wake up** to an inner vitality, whereas Michael uses meditation to **calm down**. Somewhere in between is a balance that will be just right for your needs.

Meditating can act as an internal pressure-relief valve to help you find calm *before* an explosion occurs. Releasing stress through meditation can improve your general physical and mental health by:

- reducing insomnia;
- normalizing blood pressure;
- reducing heart disease, depression, and anxiety; and
- lessening the use of cigarettes and alcohol.

When your mind settles down there is often an inner clarity, vitality, creativity, and freshness.

Meditation Express will lead you to an overall state of integration and coherence, and to the discovery and unfolding of your full potential without stress.

Whether you choose to meditate with the intention of improving your health, letting off steam, or contemplating an expanded awareness, *Meditation Express* takes you on a journey where getting there is more than half the fun.

We were serious when we said at the opening of this introduction that anyone can meditate. You just need a few tips.

Our "Top 10" List for Your Meditation Success

10. Meditate anywhere, anytime.

9. Be yourself.

8. Use only the meditations that appeal to you.

7. Be physically comfortable.

6. This is a practice—you don't have to be perfect.

5. If you start to feel frustrated because your mind absolutely refuses to slow down, stop and try again some other time.

4. Trust your intuition, but don't give up your day job.

3. Be aware of your breathing, but don't hyperventilate.

2. There's no right or wrong way to meditate.

1. *Remember to meditate!*

How to Use This Book

Once you've read the first three chapters that cover our basics of meditation, there's no right or wrong way to use this book. You may read it from beginning to end or open it randomly and trust that whatever you need will be what you've opened to. There's no specific order that you must follow. Unlike most meditation tomes that suggest that you set aside a specific time and find a quiet place each day to meditate, we urge you to **just do it**!

No Time Like the Present

Meditation is the search engine of the soul.

The volume and speed of our mind chatter can make the Internet look like a kiddie pool.

Meditation is a practice (yes, a discipline, too) that enables you to find and follow your own path through the busy-ness of your mind. The following meditations are about observing your mind chatter.

The Chatterbox Café

"Meditation: it's not what you think."

—SIGN OUTSIDE OF BAREFOOT BOB'S RESTAURANT
IN KEY WEST, FLORIDA

Exercise 1: Remember that there is no right or wrong way to do this.

> **Mx**
>
> Sit quietly for one minute (time it, an egg timer will work) and observe all the places your mind goes.

Were you aware you had so many thoughts? What were your observations? Where did your thoughts take you?

Think Pink

"Ninety percent of the game is half mental."
— Yogi Berra

Exercise 2: Here's a bit of direction for your thoughts.

> **Mx**
>
> For one minute (time it!) think of a pink elephant.

Have 60 seconds ever felt that long before? This exercise is meant to reaffirm how long a minute really is.

Don't Think Pink

"Inaction may be the highest form of action."

— JERRY BROWN

Exercise 3: Now give this a try.

Were you able to control your thoughts for one minute? Most people find it difficult to not think of something they've just been told *not* to think of!

In doing these three exercises, you've just observed that your mind has a mind of its own. Congratulations!

Now that you've observed what's going on *all the time* in your mind, you can do something about it. And don't worry if your mind wanders, even experienced meditators sometimes find these exercises extremely difficult.

Meditation is called a *practice* because it's just that. With *practice*, every time you notice your thoughts wandering, you will be able to gently bring them back on track.

Wake Up!

"The gift is in the present."
— BUMPER STICKER

If you thought meditation was only about relaxing and slowing down—get ready for a new cup of coffee! **Meditation is about waking up to what's happening around you, to what's happening inside you.** Here's another minute meditation to help you do just that.

> **Mx**
>
> Take a deep breath and bring your thoughts to the present moment. Look and really see what's around you. Make eye contact with people you meet. Focus on the temperature, lighting, colors, sounds, and smells near you. *Be present, aware, and alert!*

This meditation can be done for one minute or all the time, anytime. This is the one meditation you can use while driving (but keep your eyes open!).

Snap to It

Yogi Berra was asked what time it was, and he answered, "You mean now?"

You'll be surprised how much of the time your thoughts are not focused on what's going on in the present moment. If you're doing one task but thinking about something that happened three hours ago, you're not present!

(For this exercise you'll need to wear a rubber band on your wrist.)

> **Mx**
>
> From time to time throughout the day, stop and notice where your thoughts are. If they're stuck in the past or future, **snap the rubber band** and bring your thoughts to the present moment.

By practicing this meditation, you won't miss out on what's really going on. Now.

Track No. 9

"Even if you are on the right track, you will get run over if you just sit there."

— WILL ROGERS

A simple way to focus your thoughts and relax your body is to pay attention to your own breathing.

> **Mx**
>
> Several times a day stop whatever you are doing and take nine gentle, deep breaths. Take light, flowing, even breaths. Listen to your own breath, but breathe quietly (so that a person next to you cannot hear you). Allow your breath to slow down.

This is one of our most prescribed meditations because it is so effective.

Summary

We've explored a very important part of you: your mind. Your thoughts and intentions are what motivate you. They can also be a big distraction. New meditators can become frustrated and angry when they become aware of how often their minds wander if they've heard the myth that in meditation one's mind is supposed to become totally blank. Most everyone's mind has a tendency to wander in meditation, and that's okay. Meditating is like walking a dog that wants to race off to follow every scent it smells. Your job is to keep bringing the dog (your thoughts) back onto the sidewalk.

Our runaway thoughts are usually taking us back to the past (going over old situations, replaying old tapes) or leaping into the future (planning ahead or worrying). Any wonder we feel stressed?

However, being in the right place at the right time—when everything flows magically and smoothly—is a product of having our attention in the present moment. When you are focused on the present, you'll find that you have fewer missed opportunities and more favorable outcomes.

With practice, you *will* be able to focus and stay in the present moment.

2

Getting a Grip

Above Michael's desk is a note to himself that reads: Focus . . . Breathe . . . Pay Attention!

If you find that your thoughts wander and it's difficult to stay focused while you're meditating, that's okay. Distractions and intruding thoughts are inevitable, whether you're focusing on pink elephants or balancing your checkbook. The phone, the kids, coworkers, and your own thoughts are always interrupting.

Because we're usually pressed for time, most of us have become accustomed to doing two or more tasks simultaneously:

- Catching up on reading while eating.

- Watching TV and doing the dishes.

- Talking on the phone while driving.

It's no wonder that our minds don't want to slow down in meditation and focus on just one thought at a time! While multitasking might *seem* like a time-saving device, most often it's like eating crackers while whistling—neither task works out quite right.

Practicing meditation will help you in daily activities by making it easier to keep your mind on the present and focus on one task at a time, thereby allowing you to do a more complete and thorough job. You'll find that:

- you'll retain more of what you read,

- your dishes will be cleaner, and

- you'll complete more tasks in a shorter period of time.

It's the *practice* of observing your thoughts and choosing not to focus on the distractions that is what meditation is all about. There's an old joke that asks, "How do you get to Carneige Hall?" The answer is, "Practice, practice, practice." The same answer applies to successful meditation. Anytime you notice that your thoughts have wandered, rather than getting angry and frustrated (a distraction in itself), just gently return your attention to your original focus. It's okay if that happens again and again.

The meditations in this chapter will help you to focus and prioritize where you want to put your attention. In meditation, having a one-track mind is the key!

Focus Pocus

"How can you think and hit at the same time?"
— Yogi Berra

This exercise will make you aware of how often your focus is fragmented during your day.

> **Mx**
>
> Make a list. Each time during the day when you find yourself doing more than one task, take a minute to write down the things you're doing simultaneously.

At the end of the day, review your list. How many times was your focus fractured?

Train of Thought

"I was trying to daydream, but my mind kept wandering."

> —STEVEN WRIGHT, FROM *THE APPOINTMENTS OF DENNIS JENNINGS*

This is it—the crux of why meditation is called a *practice*.

Mx

Pick a thought, any thought, with the intention of focusing on it for one minute. Be aware of other thoughts that arise, but don't allow them to sidetrack you. Gently but firmly steer your attention back on track to your original thought.

The more you practice, the easier this becomes.

Stream of Consciousness

*"We know the human brain is a device to keep the
ears from grating on one another."*

— PETER DeVRIES

If you still can't concentrate because your mind is just
too jam-packed with thoughts, here's a practical meditation to lessen your mental pollution.

> **Mx**
>
> Imagine a rushing mountain stream flowing through
> your mind. Every time a new thought enters your
> mind, throw it into the stream and watch it flow away
> from you.

Notice how your eyes, head, and neck feel after you do
this. Releasing mental debris can also enhance how you
feel physically.

Meteor Showers

"When you sit with a nice girl for two hours you think it's only a minute. But when you sit on a hot stove for a minute, you think it's two hours. That's relativity."

—ALBERT EINSTEIN

Having a sense of abundance of time is almost nonexistent in our busy culture, which is constantly urging us to hurry up. To get a grip on managing your time, start your morning shower with this meditation. It's one of our all-time favorites and is repeated throughout this book, with different variations.

> **Mx**
>
> As you stand under the water, feel yourself being showered with an abundance of time. Lather yourself with the luxury of a sense of timelessness.

We often remind ourselves that time and clocks are a man-made invention. Have you ever seen a bird with a wristwatch?

Wake Up Now!

"Life is what happens when you're busy making other plans."

—JOHN LENNON

You can't be in two places at the same time. Being scattered among past, present, and future thoughts is an easy way to find yourself absent when opportunity knocks. This affirming meditation will help you wake up and smell the coffee.

Mx

Repeat the following sentence to yourself at least six times, becoming more emphatic with each repetition. Keep your attention focused on the words:

I am now in the present moment.

I am now in the present moment.

I am now in the present moment.

I am now in the present moment.

I am now in the present moment.

I am *now* in the present moment.

Affirmations, or assertions of positive intent, are an effective and powerful way to focus your mind. We'll discuss this more in Chapter 12.

Summary

Being able to focus your attention on the task at hand, in the present moment, is one of the goals and benefits of practicing meditation.

The exercises in this chapter have shown you how to discipline your thoughts, which will probably *always* try to wander. Your job in meditation is to keep bringing them back into focus.

Learning to use any new tool takes patience. Be gentle with yourself.

3

Soul Training

You are a package deal.

You have:

- a **mind**, often with a mind of its own, as you observed in the last chapters;

- a **heart** that can dream, burst, beat, murmer, throb, attack, and feel; and

- a **body** that is a physical structure with its own insights and wisdom.

Behind the scenes of this package is your soul: your center, core, root, essence, foundation.

Our culture validates the output of the mind more than the heart and body, leaving us all rather lopsided and top-heavy. The more out of balance you become, the more difficult it is to get in touch with your center.

Meditation is a way to re-member all the parts of yourself: to link your mind with your heart and gut feelings, in perfect balance. In meditation, with your attention focused inward, you are able to find your own place of center and serenity: your soul.

The theme of this book is for you to be able to use meditation to find your own center and to avoid the see-saw of high highs and low lows in all facets of life—in business, housework, and relationships. The theme of combining your mind, heart, and body to find your soul's truths is the foundation for many of the meditations we recommend here.

Finding your center, or centering, enables you to join and balance your mind's intellect and creativity with your heart's love with your body's wisdom.

When you're centered you'll find that:

- you are able to stay present and focus on the task at hand;

- you are able to trust your intuition, instincts, and gut feelings;

- your body is relaxed and in a state of ease; and

- you'll be in the right place at the right time.

Michael uses centering as a tool to keep himself present and focused. He uses it as a power tool to find the place—almost instantly—where he's in control. He doesn't let himself get pulled off center by swirling insanity or let past or future events pull him out of the present moment. Being centered enables him to make decisions regarding those events, but from the present moment. Being present gives Michael the benefit of utilizing the clarity of his *full* attention to attend to the task at hand.

Nancy uses a centering meditation to start her day from a place of balance, to put her in the flow.

The meditations in this chapter will **wake you up** to remembering and utilizing your innate sense of balance amid life's extremes. All you need to do is:

- be present,

- pay attention, and

- practice.

Finding your center is a way to balance yourself, to stay present and find the peaceful coexistence between opposites.

Try it for yourself, you'll like it!

Your way	*My way*
Past	*Future*
Right	*Wrong*
True	*False*
Inside	*Outside*
Left brain	*Right brain*
Top	*Bottom*
Hot	*Cold*
Giving	*Receiving*
Inhaling	*Exhaling*
Logical	*Illogical*
Fear	*Trust*

CENTER

The Center Line

"I want to find the center of me."
—Marilyn Monroe

If you often feel pushed and pulled in a zillion directions, this is the best meditation for getting yourself together and finding your center. With practice, this meditation becomes almost automatic. Anytime you feel your seesaw start to tip, go to your center line.

Remember, as a kid, drawing "connect the dots?" In this meditation, use your imagination and intention to make your connections between the dots. You may want to use the image of golf balls, diamonds, or bagels as your dots.

> **Mx**
>
> Take a gentle, deep breath; exhale. Imagine a dot in the *center* of your head, throat, chest, ribs, belly, and at the base of your spine. Take six deep breaths. With each breath, imagine you are connecting these dots, joining all parts of you in perfect balance.

You'll find that this meditation also centers you in the present moment: equidistant between the past and the future. It's that easy.

Acorns to Oaks

"Half our life is spent trying to find something to do with the time we have rushed through life saving."
— WILL ROGERS

This next meditation takes the center line one step deeper. If you're always on the run, this will help you to put down roots and get grounded for a few minutes.

Mx

Connect the dots of your center line and take a moment to feel your own inner balance. Now imagine your center line branching at the base of your spine and traveling down the center of both of your legs and out your feet, sending roots down into the earth. Wiggle your toes and feel yourself drawing nourishment up your legs and then up your center line.

Notice how your body feels when it is centered and grounded.

Eye of the Hurricane

"Amid the whirlwind of each chaotic moment, there is a quiet, peaceful center. . . . Awaken this center and you'll discover peace of mind, abundant joy, unlimited satisfaction and freedom from anxiety."

—RAM DASS

Just as a hurricane has a calm eye at its center, you, too, have a peaceful center within you.

This meditation won't change anything that's going on around you. What it will do is help you maintain your own calm while all about you chaos reigns. Do this meditation anytime outside pressures demand too much.

Mx

Connect your center line and ground yourself. With each breath, imagine that your center line and grounding lines are getting bigger. Expand your center and grounding lines equally, filling your entire body until you feel totally balanced from front to back, top to bottom, left to right, inside to outside.

Hold that thought!

Inner Sanctuary

"Stop the World, I Want to Get Off."

—TITLE OF 1961 BROADWAY PLAY BY ANTHONY
NEWELY/LESLIE BRICUSSE

This meditation will help you find a safe haven within you where you can go for an interlude of serenity and calm in the midst of total chaos and insanity. You can do this as a preventive measure or when all else has failed, as a one-minute, meditative 911.

> **Mx**
>
> Breathing deeply and slowly, center and ground yourself. Imagine that you are walking down an inner staircase into a place of ultimate serenity. With each step, feel yourself becoming more tranquil. When you step off the bottom step, take a moment to absorb the quietude. When you're ready, slowly ascend back up the steps, aware that you may return easily any time.

Know that this place will always be available to you to soothe your soul.

Soul Training

"Skeptic: someone who won't take know for an answer."

— ANONYMOUS

Once your mind, heart, and body are connected and grounded, your meditations often will lead you to profound and practical insights: your own truths. With practice, you will experience the soundness of trusting in yourself.

So, no more shoulda, woulda, couldas. This meditation will be like having your own personal soul trainer.

> **Mx**
>
> Center and ground yourself. With each breath, inhale a sense of trust, assurance, acceptance, confidence, and belief in yourself. Exhale all doubt, indecision, misgivings, and apprehensions.

Observe how you feel as you center yourself in trust.

Summary

"Soul training" helps you to connect with your center—your own place of balance, wholeness, and trust. Now that your mind, heart, and body are connected, working as a team and ready for action, all you have to do is be present and practice, practice, practice.

Just remember the following recipe for successful centering.

Basic ingredients:

1. Breathe,

2. Connect your center line,

3. Get grounded, and

4. Trust yourself.

Mix well and let set for a minute or two. Anytime you get stuck, frazzled, or off balance reuse these basic ingredients. Enjoy.

4

Trust Fund

Trust me, you'll like it.

Trust: *Belief in and reliance on the integrity, strength,
ability, surety of a person or thing.*

— Random House Dictionary

Intuition: *Direct perception of truth, independent of any
evident reasoning process; a keen and quick insight.*

— Random House Dictionary

The first few chapters in this book have introduced you to centering and several other important tools to use while meditating. This chapter is about using and trusting all of them simultaneously to access the richest tool of all: your intuition.

We have all experienced a sense of a strong inner knowing, or "gut feeling," that did not come from our five physical senses. Your intuition is your own inner truth, that which resonates within *you* as being true. Many times referred to as a "sixth sense," our intuition is a profound and powerful tool. But precisely because it cannot be described or proved to exist in a logical manner, we have learned to doubt, or not trust, our own intuitive inner wisdom.

Your inner voice of self-doubt is like the villain (in old, silent movies) who tied the hero or heroine to the railroad tracks. He's usually accompanied by the three archenemies, Shoulda, Woulda, and Coulda, and they all attempt to rob you of your faith in your intuition: your inner trust fund.

The meditations in this chapter help you renew and restore your trust in the inner whisperings of your intuition.

Magic Wand

"What is reality, anyway? Nothing but a collective hunch."

—JANE WAGNER, FROM *THE SEARCH FOR SIGNS OF INTELLIGENT LIFE IN THE UNIVERSE*

Many of us feel fragmented and have lost or forgotten the connection among our mind, body, and soul. We have come to mistrust, or we fail to recognize, our intuition. Your intuition is always within you—you need only to reestablish your lines of communication with it. Your imaginary center line that you first used in Chapter 3 is the magic wand that lets you access the innate wisdom and truth within you. Use this variation to rebuild trust in your intuition.

Mx

Imagine a star at the center of your head, heart, and the base of your spine. Starting at your heart, use your breath to connect the stars in a straight line. (On the inhale extend a line from your heart up to

continued

your head. On the exhale, extend a line from your
heart down to the base of your spine.) With each
breath, open and strengthen your lines of
communication with the magic within you: your
intuition.

The magic is within you. You just have to stay connected
with it.

Metamorphosis

"If you build it, he will come."

— William P. Kinsella, from *Shoeless Joe*

Tuition is derived from the late Middle English *tuicion*, which meant looking after, guarding. Intuition, then, is your own inner trustee.

A dramatic example of trusting and following one's intuition is the caterpillar that spins a cocoon to later emerge as a beautiful butterfly. Trusting the part of yourself that is always looking after and guarding you—your intuition—can lead you to an equally dramatic personal metamorphosis.

> **Mx**
>
> Imagine being in a cocoon that is beginning to open. Breathe deeply and feel the wings unfolding and opening within you. Sense your intuition waking up and emerging, becoming stronger with each breath.

Experience the strength and new beginnings being revealed within you.

Hello, I Know You're in There

*"Jazz will endure just as long as people hear it
through their feet instead of their heads."*

— JOHN PHILIP SOUSA

Your intuition may impart its wisdom to you in a variety of ways. It comes from your center, so there's no right or wrong way for it to divulge its insights to you. Some people actually *hear* it (as a small voice). Others *see* an image in their mind's eye (an in-sight), *feel* a sensation in their body, *smell* a fragrance, or just sense a *knowing* of their truth.

Intuition is always the very first thought or impulse that comes to you when you are centered. Trust it (within reason, please)!

> **Mx**
>
> Make a list. For one entire day, notice how many ways and times you receive intuitive messages. Take a minute to write them down.

Does your logical mind trust or reject these messages?

Trust Fund

"Trust everybody, but cut the cards."
—FINLEY PETER DUNNE

If you find it difficult to trust and act on your intuition's promptings, you're not alone. Our society places much emphasis on specialists and experts and makes trusting *yourself* an arduous task.

Learning to trust yourself is one of the richest endowments you can give yourself. This is a meditation that you can bank on!

> **Mx**
>
> Breathe in a sense of depositing strength, esteem, respect, and trust in yourself. Exhale any withdrawals of self-doubt. Feel the richness of building trust in yourself.

We often joke that we have our own personal trust fund: we *trust* ourselves that we will pull ourselves out of any hole, and we *trust* that our intuition will guide us to action.

Royal Proclamation

"Never put your trust in slogans."

— SLOGAN

Listening to your intuition is like making a royal declaration of trust in yourself.

The more you practice (notice a theme here?) trusting your intuition, the easier and more fruitful it becomes. Start off small and learn to build the foundation of trusting your intuition.

Mx

It's simple to incorporate your intuition into your daily activities. Close your eyes and ask your intuition for specific help in deciding any of the following:

- what to wear,
- what to eat,
- what to buy, and
- which route to take.

The *first* answer is usually from your intuition.

You will need to balance your intuitive insights with practicality, but be sure to trust what your intuition tells you.

Artichoke Hearts

"Believe It or Not"

— TITLE OF SYNDICATED NEWSPAPER FEATURE BY
ROBERT LEROY RIPLEY

If you're encountering static or interference while trusting your intuitive whispers, this meditation will help you get to the heart of the matter.

Focus and attention are important aspects of this meditation.

Mx

Ask yourself a question about an existing problem.
Imagine your problem in the form of an artichoke
that is in front of you. Focus your attention entirely
on the leaves of the artichoke and slowly peel them
away, one leaf at a time, until you reveal the center of
the artichoke: the heart of the matter. Your answer is
there. (If you don't sense an answer, do this
meditation several more times over the next few
days. The answer *will* reveal itself to you.)

Trust it.

Summary

The more you allow yourself to access your intuition, the more you'll learn to trust it. Your trust fund gains value and interest the more you use it. Deposits gain interest!

But now that we've encouraged you to access and trust your intuition, it doesn't mean you have to give up your logical mind or your day job. There's an old saying, "Trust in Allah, but tether your camel."

Finding a balance between your intuition and your logical mind—and then trusting it—is a rich resource.

5

Well, Well, Well

A minute a day keeps the doctor away.

We already know that meditation in itself relieves stress, which is a contributing factor to many illnesses. This chapter takes meditation to the next level, where you intentionally use your focus and attention to support your body's infinite healing resources.

If you've ever felt your heart race and your palms sweat while watching a scary movie or just thinking of a frightening incident, you've experienced a mind-body connection. Your body will have the same dramatic *but positive* physiological responses when you focus on restorative, healthful images. Your thoughts do affect your immune and endocrine systems and actually flow into every cell throughout your body. The old adages of being "only as old as you feel," "worried sick," or having a "heartwarming experience," are now being proved to be valid by the new science of psychoneuroimmunology (easier studied than said).

Health and healing are not just the absence of illness but also a sense of balance, wellness, vitality, and peace. Building on the centering and balancing concepts throughout this book, the meditations in this chapter **wake you up** to your innate healing abilities and to the active role you can play in creating and maintaining good health.

Catching Some Eee's

Balance equals ease, and imbalance equals dis-ease. This is a quick and potent elixir to help bring you back into balance.

> ### Mx
>
> Close your eyes and imagine a sense of ease flowing through you. Imagine all dis-ease, dis-comfort, and tension flowing out of your hands and feet. Breathe in and fill yourself with a palpable sense of ease.

Ease can be contagious! Not only will you be able to feel a change, others will, too. Projecting your ease can help calm a harried supermarket checkout person, a worried client, a frustrated spouse, or an angry child. But, most important is that *you'll* feel good.

Garden Variety Meditation

*"I planted some bird seed. A bird came up. Now I
don't know what to feed it."*

— UNKNOWN

Meditation is very similar to gardening: you can cultivate and nurture thoughts that are harmonious and
healthful, and weed out thoughts that are stressful or
fearful. You may also fertilize the ground and plant the
seeds of health for yourself.

This meditation sends very powerful messages to
your body's healing systems and can have profound
results when done right before sleep.

Mx

Make a list of any unhealthy "weeds" that you want to
pull from your garden (illness, smoking, junk food,
anger) and a list of "seeds" (exercise, laughter,
health, and vitality) that you want to plant. Envision
yourself standing in a garden:

- Notice its size, shape, layout, lighting, smells,
  colors.

continued

- Is it orderly or in need of attention?

- Are there things already growing?

Begin to gently pull out any weeds (make sure to get the roots), and prepare the earth for planting. After planting your new seeds, give them whatever nourishment they need.

Do this meditation several nights in a row, and watch your garden grow.

Paging Dr. You

"Early to bed, and early to rise, makes a man healthy, wealthy, and wise."

—BENJAMIN FRANKLIN

The term *doctor* is from the Latin *docere*, which means to teach. The intent of this meditation is to introduce you to the doctor, or teacher, that resides within you. Very often, a dis-ease manifests as a way to show you where you have become unbalanced or where there is an area that needs attention. In this meditation, your body teaches, or imparts, its needs to you, which you can then use when consulting with other members of your health care crew. (Again, trust your inner healer, but don't forget logic. Make use of the best medical care available!)

"So, what's up, Doc?" Bugs Bunny asked a wonderful question. Now it's your turn. You're the best specialist when it comes to your own body. So don your white coat and stethoscope, and ask your inner physician to listen to what your body wants to tell you.

Mx

Close your eyes and center yourself. Focus your attention inward to an area of discomfort and ask what it is that your body wants to tell you. Listen. You may want to ask questions:

- What do you need to feel better?

- What will bring you back into balance?

- What treatment would be most beneficial?

- Which health care providers need to be included?

These questions are just some of the questions that we recommend you ask. Trust that you'll know your own questions, as well as the answers.

Aaah Choose

"Accentuate the Positive"

—SONG TITLE BY JOHNNY MERCER/
HAROLD ARLEN

We all are free to choose where we focus our attention. Harnessing your innate abilities to focus on what's right as opposed to what's wrong with you is taking a positive, proactive role in your own health maintenance. Choosing to accentuate the positive (aaah) over the negative (grrr) adds an additional dimension to your health and vitality.

> **Mx**
>
> Find five things in your life that you can say a heartfelt "aaah . . ." about. Take a deep breath in, and on the exhale, say "aaah." Repeat for a minimum of five breaths. (For increased benefits, don't limit yourself to only five aaahs.)

You may soon become a wizard of aaahs!

Give Peace a Chants

"Give Peace a Chance"

— SONG TITLE BY LENNON/MCCARTNEY

You may want to do this meditation in a private place, such as the shower, a car, or a closet (only kidding).

We use chants to inject an antidote of serenity into our hectic days. You will discover your own methods of chanting. Experiment with what is comfortable for you. It's not the quality of your voice but the quality of the words and your attention that count.

> **Mx**
>
> For one minute, verbally repeat or sing a phrase that resonates with calm and tranquillity for you. Here are some suggestions. "Blue water, white sand, and me . . . Blue water, white sand, and me. . . ." "All is well . . . All is well . . . All is well. . . ." "May peace prevail on earth . . . May peace prevail on earth. . . ."

Before long, you'll be *chanting in the rain, just chanting in the rain* . . . and maybe even breaking into song.

Finding Your Keys

"An apple a day keeps the doctor away."

— PROVERB

Each one of us holds within ourselves individual keys, our own truths, to maintaining health and balance in our lives. Most keys are simple to find, but very often this is easier said than done. If taking care of all of your daily, routine tasks leaves you depleted, you may not even remember what it is that gives you a sense of vitality and wellness.

One of the keys that works for both of us is living in Key West, Florida. Several of Michael's keys include cooking, laughing, and taking time to say "thank you" to himself and others. Nancy needs to take a daily walk, get enough sleep, and listen to her food cravings (within balance).

This meditation will help you rediscover what *your* keys are to maintaining health and vitality, not only in your body, but also in your mind, spirit, and emotions.

> **Mx**
>
> *Make a checklist for yourself.* Sit quietly and take a
> deep breath. Ask yourself what's vital to keeping
> yourself in balance. Write down whatever comes to
> you.

You may want to do this at the beginning of your day so
that you can incorporate and utilize as many of your
keys as possible every day.

Your Timetable

"There is more to life than increasing its speed."
—GANDHI

Are you suffering from the effects of stress because you have too much to do and not enough time to do it in? Use this meditation to take a time-out for yourself by stopping the hands of time for just a moment.

> **Mx**
>
> Picture an old-fashioned, nondigital clock in front of you. Take your finger and stop the clock's second hand. While time is literally stopped for you, breathe in a sense of calm. Feel it flow gently into your shoulders and neck. With each breath that you take, feel the rest of your body relaxing. When you are ready, let go of the clock's second hand.

Be present, alert, and aware that you *do* have control over your time.

Summary

Taking a minute in the middle of a hectic day to relax and rejuvenate can have profound results on your health.

Meditation is a wondrous tool for health maintenance or dis-ease prevention that can be used beneficially in conjunction with any other healing modality.

6

Mangia, Mangia!

Food for thought

Nourishing the "whole you" is often overlooked when you're busy doing things for others. Your mind and spirit, along with your body, need to be nourished in order to stay healthy, function well, and grow.

Our culture travels almost at the speed of light. Like it or not, we've become conditioned to fast food, sound bytes, and Jiffy Lube. We are assaulted on a daily basis by a barrage of reports from radio, TV, and the print media telling us what food is good or not good for us, and what will keep us healthy or make us sick. The experts who yesterday told us that eggs were beneficial now tell us that the incredible, edible egg may not be so good after all. Good fat—bad fat? Fried or baked? Do you weigh too much or not enough?

Q: What's a person to do?

A: Listen to and trust your mind, heart, and body! (Sound familiar?)

Worrying about not getting the proper diet or feeling guilty about giving in to your cravings is stressful. If you don't often indulge yourself, chances are that you've been letting your mind edit and override your intuition and your body's inner wisdom—which is *not* centered. Your intuition and food cravings are your body's way of letting you know what it needs and wants. *Use them, don't fear them!*

The balancing of your body's needs, your heart's desires, and your mind's wisdom will, with practice, help lead you to an enriching, satisfying, balanced, and healthy diet.

Using the tool of meditation, you can be present and alert to the tastes, textures, colors, and smells of what your body needs for its healthy fulfillment. Learning to know and trust your body's signals balances the mind-body equation.

Taking a minute to meditate and center yourself during a hectic day is in itself nourishing, and it's easy, fortifying, and low calorie, too!

This chapter will show you how to use the *practice* of meditation to find your own ways to nourish your mind, body, heart, and soul. The meditations will whet your appetite, enrich your life, and **wake you up** to feeding your body and soul.

These meditations are sensible and easy. Some are for planning, preparing, and eating your meals. Others are for your pure enjoyment, to rejuvenate and refresh your whole self. They will make your heart sing, your spirit soar, your mind expand, and your body feel good.

Conscious Eating
Part I: Meal Planning

"Part of the secret of success in life is to eat what you like and let the food fight it out inside."

— MARK TWAIN

Even if you don't have a lot of time for meal preparation and planning, you can use this meditation to broaden your horizons (but not your hips), while adding variety and panache to your meals. Start this meditation without thinking of limitations (time, money, calories, etc.).

Mx

Focus your attention on the area around your navel. Take a deep breath and ask yourself this question: "If I could eat anything in the world right now, what would it be?" Acknowledge the first concept that comes to you. While still in meditation, ask your mind, heart, and body to work together to show you a balanced, healthy, and feasible way to satisfy your cravings with the demands of the real world.

If you crave a dish that includes mushrooms, but no one else will eat them, cook the dish with the mushrooms on the side.

Conscious Eating
Part II: Digging In

"I've been on a diet for two weeks and all I've lost is two weeks."

— TOTIE FIELDS

This meditation can be done whether you're eating fast food or slow food, standing, sitting, eating alone or with others. You may choose to do this for one minute or for an entire meal.

Mx

Bring your thoughts and full attention to the food in front of you, and before you start to eat, observe your food as if you're seeing it for the first time. Begin eating, noticing the smells and colors, feeling the texture and temperature of the food, savoring each bite. Notice what part of your tongue tastes the food. Wait a moment after swallowing before continuing. STOP eating when you are aware you are full.

Making the effort to spend quality time with your food is a lot like taking time to smell the roses. Practiced frequently, this meditation will assist you in shedding (or gaining) a few pounds—effortlessly!

The Zen of Carrot Peeling

"I was a vegetarian for a while, but I quit because it has side effects. I found myself sitting in my living room, starting to lean towards the sunlight."

—RITA RUDNER

Our dear friend, Deborah, told us that her first experience of the "zen" of meditation occurred unexpectedly in her kitchen over 20 years ago while she was peeling carrots.

We offer this meditation as a way to add zest to your culinary tasks.

> ## Mx
>
> The next time you peel a vegetable (or do any "mundane" job), put your *full attention* on the task at hand. Instead of rushing to complete the task, be aware of every movement you make. Observe the details: the smells, colors, textures, lighting, and beauty around you. Savor the complexity and the simplicity of your task.

This is also how Michael uses cooking as a meditation to switch from his work mode to a more relaxed pace. By focusing fully on each step of preparing a meal, instead of replaying business meetings or phone calls in his head, he clears his mind of his daily clutter. He's able to truly leave the office when he leaves the office.

Guiltless Indulgence

"Too much of a good thing can be wonderful."

— MAE WEST

Our definition of the word *indulgence* is to be benignly permissive, while keeping a sense of balance in mind.

Start by taking a full two minutes to indulge and treat yourself to your "just desserts." Focusing on receiving graciously while meditating will help you to be kinder to yourself in your daily life. Give yourself permission to be treated well—you're worth it.

Mx

Imagine yourself entering your favorite restaurant. The maitre d' asks you, "May I take your guilt?" and proceeds to seat you at the head of a simple but elegant table. Your wish is his command, and you may ask for anything. Place your order and see it being served to you.

Bon appetit!

Choices Café

"Reminds me of my safari in Africa. Somebody forgot the corkscrew and for several days we had to live on nothing but food and water."

— W. C. Fields

If you're generally focused on getting ahead in your career or household tasks, and are busy nourishing others, you may have lost touch with the concept of feeding your own soul.

We are always making choices that either nourish or deplete our health as well as our souls.

We've created a menu of nourishing Soul Food from our own Choices Café.

Soul Food Menu

Love	Joy
Kindness	Passion
Respect	Sailing
Sleep	Nature's beauty
Laughter	Writing
Beauty	Cooking

What would be on *your* Soul Food Menu? Take a minute and list a few things that nourish your soul.

> **Mx**
>
> Close your eyes and think about the choices (not just food) that you've made in the last hour. Did they nourish you or deplete you?

Check your list. Are you getting your minimum daily requirement of Soul Food?

Renaissance Faire

"It Don't Mean a Thing if It Ain't Got That Swing"

—SONG TITLE BY DUKE (EDWARD KENNEDY) ELLINGTON

The Renaissance was a period of enlightenment and change, when people nourished their souls through creative expression.

In our information age, with computers rushing us through our days at lightning speeds, many of us have little time for creative endeavors. But we all can add a dash of nourishing creativity to even the most mundane tasks throughout the day by tapping into the wellspring of our own innate originality.

So, don your beret, slip into your dancing shoes, or pick up your baton, and take a moment to renew and revive your sense of ingenuity.

This meditation is a work in progress. Do it often.

Start this meditation at any time throughout the day when you are faced with doing an ordinary, everyday task. The meditation is to approach the task with the intention of making it an original work of art. Add your own panache and verve.

Notice how fulfilling it becomes when you make the ordinary extraordinary.

Wellness Days

"Days off."

—SPENCER TRACY, WHEN ASKED WHAT HE
LOOKED FOR IN A SCRIPT

All work and no play can make Jack and Jill very stressed out. If your days off are as busy as your workdays, you may have forgotten how to have a true "day off."

Before your stress turns into an illness, treat yourself to a wellness minute; take a moment and ask your mind, body, and heart to remember what would nourish your whole being.

> **Mx**
>
> Take a deep breath and center yourself. Ask your mind, "What would bring me joy?" Repeat this question individually to your heart and then your body. Listen for their answers.

We encourage you to incorporate some aspect of your insights into your day. Even better, don't wait to take a sick day. Enjoy a wellness day.

Guest of Honor

"Come quickly, I am tasting stars!"
—DOM PERIGNON, AT THE MOMENT OF
HIS DISCOVERY OF CHAMPAGNE

If you find yourself often giving too much to others, to the point of your own depletion, use this meditation as a quick substitute for a hot bubble bath. It only takes a minute.

Mx

As you take a gentle, deep breath, imagine a glittery sense of celebration bubbling through you, like confetti, champagne, or sparkling cider. Allow this feeling to expand, replenishing, revitalizing, and refilling you.

Celebrate yourself!

Summary

Food for thought: nourishment takes many forms. We are not just what we eat. The world abounds with beauty, humor, music, and love to nourish your body and soul. Whether it's pizza or pasta for your body, poetry or Picasso for your soul, or Rubik's cube and crossword puzzles for your mind, all parts of you need nourishment to stay healthy.

Give yourself permission to partake fully, lavishly, and graciously in the banquet of life. It only takes a minute.

7

Excess Baggage

Who needs it!

Most of us know what the term "excess baggage" means, and for the most part, we all carry some degree of it around with us wherever we go. It's usually the mind chatter that many of us experience when we meditate: the dialog or old tape that keeps playing about events from our past or events yet to come. It's very hard to stay present when old thoughts, patterns, and tapes—or new fears, worries, and projections—keep playing in your mind.

Excess baggage is the stuff that can make you angry and frustrated and keep you from being aware of the present moment!

Excess baggage comes in many varieties and forms, from a three-piece set to an 18-piece ensemble. Carrying old emotions (guilt, fear and anger, grief) can become burdensome and even affect your physical body in the form of a stiff neck, tense shoulders, and a sore back. The list in itself is fatiguing.

The meditations in this chapter will help **wake you up** to ways to shed extra baggage—whether it's in your mind, your emotions, or your body. (Who knows, they might even help with the clutter in your closets!)

Baggage Claims

"I'm Gonna Wash That Man Right Outa My Hair"
— FROM THE MUSICAL *SOUTH PACIFIC*

Do you know how much old fear, angst, guilt, anger, grief, worry, responsibility, or jealousy is stored in your baggage compartment?

A sure way to shed some of this excess baggage is to first know how to acknowledge and identify it. You'll need a pen and paper for this meditation.

> **Mx**
>
> Focus your attention on your center line, but also allow yourself to be distracted by any thoughts that appear. Any time your thoughts start to wander, jot down the thought, then go back to focusing on your center line. Repeat, continuing to write down every intruding thought.

What are your most prevalent intruding thoughts? If you'd like to unload some of them, the following meditations will show you how.

Blown in the Wind

His absence is good company.

—Scottish saying

If anything on your list from the previous meditation pertains to anger, this meditation is a good way to vaporize it.

Mx

Close your eyes and take a deep breath (exhaling any steam if necessary). Take one of the things on your list that angers you and direct that angry thought into one of your hands. Close your hand tightly, and direct all of your focus into that hand, pulverizing the anger into dust. Open your hand and blow away the dust.

Repeat the same process for each of your intruding, angry thoughts.

Un-Backpacking

"I like a woman with a head on her shoulders. I hate necks."

—Steve Martin

If your excess baggage makes you feel like Atlas, with the responsibility of the world on your shoulders, this meditation will lighten your load.

It is particularly helpful if some of your excess baggage includes the inability to say "no" to others.

> **Mx**
>
> Focus your attention on your neck, shoulders, and upper back. Place your hands on the muscles between your neck and shoulders, and alternately knead those muscles. With each breath, feel the weight of one of the outdated responsibilities on your list being lifted off of your shoulders. Do this for as long as your list, or your time, permits.

Take a minute to knead your shoulder muscles just for the pleasure of it.

Held Up? Hand It Over

*"Start every day off with a smile and get it over
  with."*

— W. C. FIELDS

This meditation is a handy way to release old baggage
that is full of "toxic," entangling emotions. Relief is literally at your fingertips—FAST. Each finger represents
a specific emotional release—there's a chart on the next
page to help you remember.

You can do this detox anytime, at a stoplight, before
bed, or while you're washing your hands.

> **Mx**
>
> With your left hand, grasp your right thumb and hold
> it for a moment. Gently pull out imaginary cobwebs
> of worry from your thumb. Hold each of your fingers
> individually, pulling out the corresponding emotional
> cobweb (see chart). As you pull out each cobweb,
> allow your finger to be filled with a sense of freedom,
> vitality, and refreshment. Repeat the process with
> your other hand.

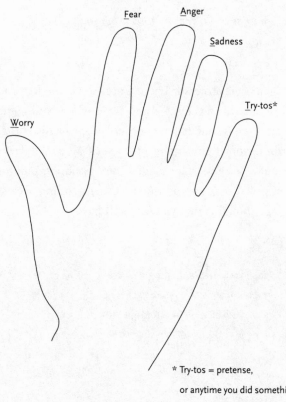

Fear   Anger

Sadness

Try-tos*

Worry

* Try-tos = pretense,
  or anytime you did something,
  but your heart wasn't in it.

Professor Irwin Corey's Magnets

"Go, and never darken my towels again."
—Groucho Marx

Octogenarian professor Irwin Corey is a comedian and philosopher from the 1960s and 1970s who is still going strong. One of our favorite observations of his is that lightbulbs don't emit light—they suck all of the darkness out of a room! This meditation has similar pull for helping you to let go of any of your intruding, excess baggage thoughts that you may still have.

> **Mx**
>
> Close your eyes and imagine a crane with a giant magnet (the kind used to pick up and move junk cars). Feel all of your outdated thoughts and patterns being gently pulled away from you by the magnet. Allow your excess baggage to leave you, using your exhale breath to help the magnet lift away your old, rusty junk.

We find this meditation especially useful before and after family gatherings. With a little bit of practice, and a dollop of love, you'll find that letting go is not so hard to do.

Summary

It's "bad news, good news" time.

The Bad News: life is filled with distractions, and our excess baggage is only one of them.

The Good News: you've identified and learned how to release some of your old, excess baggage.

8

All You Need Is Love

What are your heart's desires?

The word *love* is used copiously—advertisers tell us we'll love our sneakers or attract love by using a certain deodorant, floor cleaner, cake mix, or kitty litter. Do we actually love our sneakers the same way we love our partners, parents, or children?

Have we forgotten what it is to genuinely love?

Historically, women have been encouraged to demonstrate love by nurturing others, and men have been directed to express love by being protectors and providers. Now that our times have given men and women the permission to do both, we believe the easiest way for everyone to express love is through simple, genuine acts of loving-kindness from your heart to convey affection, caring, and compassion to yourself and others.

Love may be expressed in infinite ways. This chapter is a Cupid's bounty of meditations that will **wake you up** to opening your heart, finding your passion, and infusing your life with love.

Love Begins at Home

"To love oneself is the beginning of a lifelong romance."

— OSCAR WILDE

Many of us find it easier to give love than to receive it, often to the extreme of self-denial when it comes to nurturing ourselves. Who hasn't been told that it's better to give than to receive?

This meditation nurtures the nurturer.

> **Mx**
>
> Put your hand on your forehead and feel the warmth or the coolness of your own hand comforting you. When you inhale, imagine a stream of love entering your nose and then filling your chest. Continue this for several more breaths.

Feel the love nurturing and revitalizing you.

This Bud's for You

"I kissed my first girl and smoked my first cigarette on the same day. I haven't had time for tobacco since."

— ARTURO TOSCANINI, CONDUCTOR

If it feels like it's been a long time since you've felt your own heart's love, this meditation is a wonderful new beginning: a nonsurgical, open-heart operation. We prescribe that you do this meditation for as many or as few breaths as time allows.

For a sensual addition, place a dab of scented oil below your nostrils for fragrance, and place your hand over your heart to feel your own heartbeat.

> **Mx**
>
> Imagine a flower bud in the center of your chest. As you take a deep breath, observe the bud opening and unfolding. (Yes, just like in time-lapse photography.) With each of your breaths, feel your chest relax.

Know that your own heart is opening and pumping love to every cell in your body.

Valentine's Day

"If love is the answer, could you please rephrase the question?"

—JANE WAGNER

The following meditation is a quick and easy refresher that can be done for one minute several times a day and gets you into the practice of being able to receive love. Taking even this short "breather" will renew and rejuvenate you.

Nurturing and remembering how to love yourself take practice . . . practice . . . practice.

> **Mx**
>
> Focus your attention on the middle of your chest. Imagine a Valentine's heart surrounded by five Cupids. With each of your next five breaths, imagine that one of the Cupids is pouring a cup of unconditional love into your heart. Accept these drinks of love.

There are no strings attached!

The Power of Love

"What's Love Got to Do with It?"

— SONG TITLE BY TINA TURNER

Writers and philosophers have stated that there are two basic motivators in your life: love and fear.

You are relaxed and "in the flow" when you're motivated by love (feeling joy, passion, enthusiasm):

- going to the gym because it makes you feel good,

- arriving at work on time because you enjoy your job and like receiving a paycheck, or

- eating well because you enjoy being healthy.

You are in a state of stress when you're motivated by fear (feeling anger, frustration, guilt):

- going to the gym because you fear you'll get fat,

- getting to work on time because you're afraid you'll get fired, or

- restricting your diet because you're afraid of becoming ill.

Realizing that you can choose what to be motivated by gives you a sense of control and offers instant stress relief.

This meditation is wonderful if you find yourself primarily motivated by fear. Take a few moments to choose to switch to an alternative energy source.

> **Mx**
>
> Inhale gently, placing your focus on your coccyx, or tail bone. Imagine there's a power plant based there, generating love up your spine and throughout your body, mind, spirit, and emotions. With each breath, feel the love energizing you. With each exhale, imagine any fear or anxiety leaving the smokestack.

It's your choice.

Heart's Desire

Bliss: rapture, delight, joy, happiness, pleasure, enchantment, elation, transport, paradise, ecstasy.

—Roget's *Thesaurus*

Many of us are so busy *thinking* or *doing* that we're listening impaired when it comes to hearing our heart's whispers.

Our logical minds usually have veto power over our heart's yearnings and wisdom, with the cynical idea that anything we love to do or eat is probably unhealthy, immoral, or illegal. And while the real world does offer some limitations on *following* your bliss, there are no limitations in meditation on *finding* your bliss.

Can you even remember your heart's desires? We all have pages of "to do" lists that occupy our days. Does anyone have a "to love" or "to enjoy" list?

This meditation can be done in one minute, at your desk or in the kitchen.

Stop for one minute and ask yourself the question: "If I could do *anything* in the world right now, without limitations, what would it be?" *Look* within and see what your heart desires. *Listen* to your inner voice and hear how you might bring this bliss into your life.

Do this often and keep a Bliss List to remind you of all of your passions.

Passion Fruit Cocktail

"Sex is good, but not as good as fresh sweet corn."

—Garrison Keillor, humorist

The recipe for this juicy meditation is:
1 part Bliss List   2 parts imagination
Shake well. Serve several times a day.

When you think of passion, do you think only of sex? Passion is also a boundless enthusiasm for food, art, humor, music, baseball . . . anything. Most of us have a secret, or not so secret, passion that we may have left by the side of the road. Do this meditation with your Bliss List in front of you to rekindle the passions in your life.

Mx

Take a gentle, deep breath. As you inhale (yes, it's okay to inhale), imagine that your breath is igniting a spark of burning desire within you. With each breath see the flame of your desire getting brighter and fuller.

Keeping your passions alive and making time for them in your daily life is a main ingredient in this healthful recipe. Notice your vitality and sense of joy increasing as your passion increases.

Love Potion No. 9

"I always wanted to be somebody, but I see now, I should have been more specific."

—JANE WAGNER, FROM *THE SEARCH FOR SIGNS OF INTELLIGENT LIFE IN THE UNIVERSE*

Learning to love and be kind to yourself is a prerequisite to finding a loving relationship. But now what? How do you find your perfect partner, your soul mate?

Making a wish list is a centuries-old idea that still works in our modern day. If you know what you want, isn't it much easier to go out and find it? But, if you're living in a whirlwind, putting everyone else's needs before your own and not checking in with your heart from time to time, your deepest desires are often forgotten. A wish list is a simple way to attract your soul mate, and it's easy and less expensive than a personals ad when combined with meditation.

Nancy used her Soul Mate Wish List with this meditation, and the result was that she met Michael! Actually . . . she had to do it twice. On her first list she was not specific enough and forgot to include that she wanted a *balanced* combination of all of the qualities, and the result was less than ideal! A glimpse of some of the highlights of Nancy's *successful* wish list are shown here:

1. Loves me!
2. Enjoys cooking
3. Is available
4. Is healthy
5. Wants to be in a monogamous relationship
6. Walks upright (not taking any chances here)
7. Chews with his mouth closed

Get the picture? Now it's your turn! Before you do the next meditation, make a list of all of the attributes that you would like to find in your soul mate, setting no limitations on your soul's desires. Take your time and give some serious and fun thought to what you ask for, because your wish might come true. Go for the "gold standard," ask for balance, and remember to *be specific*!

Our concept for this meditation is that you attract and draw into your life the things that you pay attention to.

Do this love potion meditation at least once a day with your own wish list in front of you.

Close your eyes for one minute and imagine a person who embodies all of the qualities on your wish list walking toward you. Smile and greet him or her with an open heart.

Good luck. Please let us know when you set the wedding date.

Summary

So, "what's love got to do with it"? Everything!

Unconditional love has a profound and healing effect, not just on those with whom we interact on a daily basis, but also on ourselves.

You'll be amazed how full your life will feel by stopping for just a minute or two during your day to focus on and feel love. By filling yourself with love and using love as a motivator, you are then able to radiate it outward, often creating quite a ripple effect.

We know that by practicing these meditations you will open your heart, find your passion, and infuse your life with love.

9

Get Outa Here!

Travel/Vacation

*Fun, nurturing retreats in Paradise. Beautiful lodgings
in exotic locales. Swim with dolphins, climb sacred
mountains, explore the ancient pyramids. Mouthwatering
gourmet healthy meals that shed pounds. Relax with
unlimited healing bodywork and pampering by former
Greek gods and goddesses. Nonstop first-class flights. All
inclusive via the Meditation Express. Cost: a minute*

or two in the middle of a hectic day. For more information and reservations, close your eyes and . . .

Sound too good to be true? Or are you already searching for your passport?

The workplace, your home, and the world in general can become pressure cookers filled with deadlines and responsibilities. This chapter gives you the luxury of escaping from everyday pressures, tensions, and demands, at least for a minute. We'll show you how to create a refreshing interlude—an oasis in the middle of your hectic day. You'll experience the freedom, relaxation, and refreshment of a vacation without having to plan, pack, and travel.

Nancy likes to take a preventive mini-vacation every two hours when she's working under pressure (work two hours, vacation for two minutes). When Michael feels pressured by yet another schedule, he takes his mini-vacations when he thinks he's about to blow his top.

The meditations in this chapter will take you on mini-vacations—while you're on a coffee break or on hold on the phone—and the retreats will **wake you up** to some refreshing "in-sightseeing."

Summer Soulstice

"Weather forecast for tonight: dark."
—GEORGE CARLIN

Summertime, and the living is easy. But what do you do in December when you find yourself feeling constricted by boundaries of work, time, or money?

Take this mini-vacation to the tropics to recharge your "soul-ar" batteries. This meditation uses your breath to reconnect you with the part of you that is limitless. There are *no* limitations in this meditation. Splurge and do this for two minutes.

> **Mx**
>
> With your eyes either open or closed, breathe gently into your upper abdomen, or solar plexus, imagining sunrise in a tropical island paradise. With each breath, sense the sun rising and becoming fuller, radiating warmth, light, and vitality into every cell in your body.

Absorb it!

Rushin' Roulette

"For fast acting relief, try slowing down."
— JANE WAGNER

For a new kind of vacation, this meditation gives you a different perspective on time. Try this quick getaway from your hectic pace several times a day and say aaah.

Mx

Whatever you're doing (washing dishes, walking, dialing the phone), slow your movements down to half speed for a full minute. Be aware of your movements, and make the conscious effort to slow down and focus on what you are doing. (Your mind will probably be telling you to hurry up, but tell it to take a break for just a minute!)

By slowing down and not "rushin'" we have found that we accomplish more and do a better job because we are present and focused.

Magic Carpet Ride

"Beam me up, Scotty."

—LINE FROM GENE RODDENBERRY'S *STAR TREK*

If you spend a lot of time weaving in and out of traffic (deadlines, commitments, responsibilities), here's a twist. This is the ultimate getaway—without reservation.

Your thoughts and intentions can lead you to exotic and magical destinations—intertwined with this meditation, the sky's the limit!

> ### Mx
>
> Picture a magical, flying carpet floating in front of you. Notice its color, texture, size, and shape. Climb aboard and allow the threads of your heart's desires to transport you to a place of your dreams. Escape it all for a minute.

When we don't have even a minute to do this meditation fully, we close our eyes and envision ourselves sitting atop the magic carpet, floating free with no destination in mind.

Mardi Gras

"Is this the party to whom I am speaking?"

— LILY TOMLIN AS ERNESTINE THE OPERATOR

Everyone likes a good party. Take a fiesta break in the middle of your hectic day to add some zip when your energy is failing. Just for a minute, let your hair down, take off your glasses, and loosen your necktie. The conga line is waiting as you visit the festival within you.

> **Mx**
>
> Start with a couple of deep breaths. Think of Rio, Mardi Gras, New Year's Eve, or any festive moment in your memory. Hear the music; feel the rhythm; see the costumes; enjoy the laughter, lights, balloons, sights, and smells of the festival. Be a part of it!

Warning: May cause unexpected joy and happiness, too!

Cinema Shorts

"It is through the cracks in our brains that ecstasy creeps in."

—Logan Pearsall Smith, *Afterthoughts*

Don't have time to go to a movie in the middle of your day? You can go to a minute matinee with the following meditation.

> **Mx**
>
> Close your eyes and picture yourself seated alone in the middle of a dark, quiet movie theater. The screen before you, large and silent, comes to life with a scene from your favorite movie. It is playing only for you and just as you remember it.

Use this minute to stop and smell the popcorn.

Summary

This chapter is one of our personal favorites and varies slightly from the premise of keeping you focused in the present moment. Several of the meditations add a touch of daydreaming to our prescription for stress relief, allowing you at least a moment's vacation from your fast-paced day.

10

Now I Lay Me Down to Sleep

Lullaby, and good night . . .

Ideally, nighttime is a period of renewal for your body, mind, and soul. The action and aggression of the sun and daylight are replaced by the gentle glow of the stars and reflective moonlight.

But, unfortunately, bedtime is not always a time for rest. Some of us spend a good part of this time tossing and turning, either rerunning our "movie of the day" and fighting with ourselves over a lost opportunity or worrying ourselves into a frenzy over tomorrow's activities. Instead of rest and relaxation, bedtime can become a battlefield of past and future encounters.

You can rest assured that the meditations in this chapter will not be **waking you up** as they have in the past chapters, but they *will* be bringing you back to being in the present moment. They will help to ease your transition from wakefulness to sleep and make your slumber a peaceful and rejuvenating experience.

Mental Floss

"Consciousness: that annoying time between naps."

— UNKNOWN

It's often difficult after a busy day to get your mental chatter to call it quits so that you can get some rest. As part of your nightly preparations for sleep, do this meditation as soon as you get into bed. It's as important to clean your cerebral matter as it is your teeth.

> **Mx**
>
> Take a couple of deep breaths and center yourself. Begin to list at least five things that happened during the day that you are grateful for. Whenever an "angst" thought arises, replace it with another thing that you have to be grateful for.

Instead of counting sheep, count your blessings! If you're stumped after a *really* tough day, start with the basics: 1. Having food, 2. Having shelter, 3. Getting an extra 20 miles out of your car that has 180,000 miles, and so on.

Rheostat

"The best cure for insomnia is plenty of sleep."
— W. C. Fields

If your mind is still active and refuses to let you drift off, this meditation will help you to focus on the task at hand: going to sleep!

Mx

After getting comfortable in bed, close your eyes and imagine that you have a dial that you can turn to control the volume and speed of your inner thoughts. Whenever your mental chatter pops into your mind, focus on your rheostat to turn it down—lower, lower, then off.

Night, night.

Shhhhhhh . . .

"Sleep is an excellent way of listening to an opera."
—James Stephens

We live in a noisy world. Flushing toilets, leaky faucets, traffic sounds, crickets chirping, even your beloved's snoring—all can prevent or disrupt your peaceful slumber. This is a simple and very effective meditation for finding a quiet night's sleep.

> **Mx**
>
> Get into your favorite sleeping position. Imagine you are standing at the top of a candlelit spiral staircase. With each step you descend, the outside noise that you are hearing diminishes. At the bottom of these steps is a door leading to your soundproof room of inner quiet. Open the door, step inside, and close the door behind you, shutting out all outside noises. You are now in a place of perfect inner solitude.

Sleep well.

Sleeping Den and Now

"Sometimes I wake up grumpy; other times I let him sleep."

—ANONYMOUS

Bears hibernate, cats nap, and sleeping dogs are left lying. What's their secret? Perhaps it's that they feel totally comfortable in their surroundings.

If you're often awake during the middle of the night and not able to get back to sleep, put yourself into this meditative sanctuary.

Mx

In your mind's eye, design the ultimate sleeping chamber for yourself, as opulent and safe as you desire. You can choose to be alone, or feel free to invite whomever you wish to join you. You may envision music being played, flowers, scented candles . . . Breathe deeply, and feel yourself enfolded in security and quiescence.

In this meditation there are no limitations.

Sweet Dreams

"Last night I dreamed I ate a 10-pound marshmallow, and when I woke up the pillow was gone."

— TOMMY COOPER

To put a whipped cream topping on your day, end it by programming yourself for a night's worth of sweet dreams.

> **Mx**
>
> Once in bed and comfortable, close your eyes and picture a loved one. Focus your attention on the person's features: mouth, eyes, hair. See the person smile or touch you lovingly.

Let yourself be soothed and drift off to sleep with the help of this delicious meditation.

Summary

Neither of us has much of a problem going to sleep, so the on-the-job training to get these meditations just right was exhausting: nap, write about it, nap, write about it. It was a tough job, but we persevered.

As writers, we also never thought that we'd intentionally write something that would put people to sleep. Fortunately, this chapter has changed all that.

Sweet dreams.

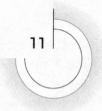

11

Meditate on This!

Who's in charge of your life?

Even the most motivated of us can get sidetracked by anger. Traffic jams; crowded elevators; confrontations with family members, coworkers, or friends can leave us angry, frustrated, and often confused. Trying to find the source of your anger can lead to an internal debate that can, if you allow it to, disrupt your entire day.

Much of the stress and frustration we experience in our daily lives is the result of feeling that we are not in control. Most anger, though, is ultimately directed at ourselves. We're ticked off that we did or didn't do or say, or should or shouldn't have done or said, something. We all need a relief valve—a way to step back and take stock of what we're feeling, what we're doing, and how we're doing it.

Striking fear into the "heart of man" is not a good thing, and if your dog and the kids start cringing when you start to bellow, it might be time for Plan B.

You can use the meditations in this chapter in the middle of a hectic day at work or at home to help you take a few minutes to let off steam, feel in control of your anger (if nothing else), and get yourself quickly back on track.

Magic Toothbrush

"Be true to your teeth or your teeth will be false to you."

— DENTAL PROVERB

Do you ever clench your jaws or grit your teeth until your whole head hurts? Or, do you clench your jaw and grind your teeth without even knowing you're doing it?

A lot of the tensions we hold in our jaws are things that we wanted to say but didn't; maybe some anger we didn't express and held back. This meditation is useful whenever you feel "spitting mad" or "like spitting bullets"—but don't.

Mx

Imagine that you have a magical toothbrush (it can be in any form) that will remove anger, tension, and frustration. With this toothbrush, start to gently brush your teeth, gums, and the roof of your mouth, letting particles and patterns of anger be brushed away.

Feel your jaw and each tooth relaxing as they release anger.

Note: A clenched jaw may lead to a clenched fist, which isn't healthy, by gum.

Bridge over Troubled Water

"Avoid fried meats which angry up the blood."

—Satchel (Leroy) Paige

Being in a perpetual state of anger can make your blood boil (into high blood pressure). It's a universal concept that forgiving yourself as well as others is a bodacious tool for letting off steam. Deciding to forgive is the hardest part.

This is a meditation to help you bridge the gap between anger and love—whether the anger is directed toward another person or yourself.

> **Mx**
>
> Imagine a rope with a knot tied in it. The knot represents something that you need to forgive in yourself or in others. Focus on the knot, and with each breath, loosen it. Feel the knot of anger within you releasing and a stream of love increasing.

Building a bridge is a large undertaking. Do this often.

Holidaze

"Control yourself: remember that anger is only one letter short of danger."

— UNKNOWN

Aaah, the holidays—family gatherings, great expectations. Or, bah, humbug! While holidays can be fun, they can also bring new meaning to the term nuclear (as in explosion) family. Certain family members may still push old buttons and ignite your verbal flamethrower.

If just saying no to the invitation is not an option, this easy centering meditation will help you to stay in a holiday mood instead of making you feel like a Scrooge.

Mx

Smile outwardly and to yourself. Center yourself from your head to your toes. With love, expand your center line to create a protective force field (as in *Star Trek* and *Star Wars*) around you. This barrier will deflect all cutting remarks, sarcasm, and pointed barbs. Stay centered, and "may the Force be with you!"

The results of this meditation can be a lot of fun, as family members who might be used to getting a rise out of you get a smile instead. More importantly, you'll feel great.

Please Release Me . . . Let Me Go

"Most folks are about as happy as they make up their minds to be."

— Abraham Lincoln

Anger is one of those intangible things that is hard to get a handle on, and dealing with it is often a difficult task. Michael tried many different methods and finally zeroed in on this meditation, which helped him to get a grip on his anger.

Mx

This can be done with your eyes either open or closed. Take two deep breaths. Imagine your anger shrunk down and small enough to fit into the palm of your hand. Close your hand into a fist and squeeze tightly. Imagine your anger getting smaller and smaller. Keep squeezing until you feel your anger lessened. Open your hand and throw away the remnants of your anger.

This meditation is very effective because it gives you the power to channel your anger into a more manageable size. It's a wonderful release.

Stop the Presses!

"When angry, count four; when very angry, swear."

— MARK TWAIN

This is another of Michael's favorite, never-fail anger diffusers. It's a grown-up version of being told to count to 10 to cool down.

> **Mx**
>
> Breathing normally, count from 1 to 30. You may either picture the numbers in your mind's eye or say the numbers to yourself. Focus on each number as you count, and think only of that number. When you get to 30, take a deep breath and count back down to number 1.

Do this whenever you feel you are about to blow your top.

Summary

By learning how to control your anger, you put yourself in charge of your own life. Letting others or outside influences push you to say or do things not in your own best interest is similar to letting a backseat driver choose your destination.

Anger is a toxic emotion that can cause physical and emotional damage to you and those around you. Using these meditations to control your anger is a gift to yourself that others will appreciate as well.

Affirmative Action

*What you pay attention to
in your life increases.*

Nancy has been teaching prosperity workshops, believing in the adage that you teach best that which you most need to learn. In this chapter she shares her ongoing experiences of moving from a "poverty mentality" (never believing that she had enough time, money, self-confidence—you name it) to an "abundance mentality" (*knowing* how to create wealth and health on many levels).

Knowing that prosperity includes but is not limited to financial abundance, Nancy shares her insights for removing limitations (financial or otherwise) and gaining freedom to fulfill your dreams. We spell *whealth* with *wh* because we feel that the term is then all-inclusive, encompassing financial, mental, emotional, and physical aspects. If your inner dialog keeps you focused on "not having enough," then that is what you will continue to manifest. If, however, your inner dialog is focused on abundance, then that is what you will experience.

Make a list of the areas in your life where you think you don't have enough, in other words, where you have a poverty mentality. For example, I don't have enough

- time,
- love,
- clothes,
- self-esteem,
- respect,
- support,
- health,
- money,

- education, or

- freedom.

Be aware of your ongoing inner dialog. Is it reinforcing your poverty mentality? If so, you can make affirmations to create an abundance mentality, *now*, in the present moment.

An affirmation is not meant to be "pie-in-the-sky," or an instant fix, but it *is* a statement of your intent.

Every day for 19 years, treasure hunter Mel Fisher affirmed to himself and his crew, "Today's the day!" It ultimately was, when he discovered the mother lode of the sunken Spanish galleon *Atocha*, valued at over $400 million.

Affirmations need to be stated in the positive and present tense (for example, "I am now creating an abundance mentality," *not* "I don't have a poverty mentality") and repeated continuously. Use an affirmation to replace any thought from your poverty mentality or to enhance your abundance mentality.

Examples:

- An abundance of time flows through me.

- I am worthy of respect and love.

- My body is now healing itself.

- I am now attracting all of the money I need and want.

- I am now free to pursue my own interests.

One of the earliest and still most effective affirmations was coined by Emile Coué, a French psychotherapist: "Every day, in every way, I'm getting better and better." He used this to heal physical ailments, but we find it to be universally applicable.

Here are some of our whealth affirmations:

- I know I can, I know I can, I know I can.

- Aaah, life is good.

- I am now rich in body, mind, and spirit.

Nancy's insights are from a woman's perspective, but this chapter is geared for anyone who has issues around prosperity, power, and wealth, or is more comfortable with giving than receiving. The meditations in this chapter include walking meditations, affirmations, and the opening of a new mind-set.

Affirmative Action

"Riches are mental, not material."
—B. C. Forbes (1880–1954)

To take your own steps for affirmative action, do this walking meditation.

> **Mx**
>
> Whether you're walking from your desk to the elevator or on a 20-minute power walk, use your inner dialog to consciously repeat any of your affirmations to yourself, instead of letting your thoughts roll into the future or back into your (former) poverty mentality.

Exercising your power of affirmative thinking is just as important as exercising your physical body. Your results will be subtle but powerful.

Golden Opportunity

"That's it, baby, if you've got it, flaunt it."
— MEL BROOKS, *THE PRODUCERS*

Keep in mind that your body cannot tell the difference between what is real or imagined and take this golden moment to feel like a million.

> **Mx**
>
> Think about how it would feel to have all the whealth, prosperity, freedom, respect, self-esteem, and time that you ever wanted. Notice how it feels to have this abundance. Does it make you smile, stand taller, breathe deeper?

If you have trouble seeing yourself in this picture, remember that creating an abundance mentality takes practice, practice, practice.

Shower of Riches

"It's delightful, it's delicious, it's de-lovely."
—Cole Albert Porter

As we told you in Chapter 2, this is a favorite meditation, with many variations. This meditation is meant to be done in the shower.

> **Mx**
>
> After you've gotten the water temperature just right, step in and imagine that you're being showered with whealth. (You may visualize money signs, $100 bills, Cupid's hearts, or health flowing over you.) Adjust the shower to cascade over you with whatever riches you desire, and let the water wash away any barriers that block you from receiving whatever you want. Breathe in a sense of abundance flowing over you.

You can never be too rich or too clean!

Independence Day

"Whoever said money can't buy happiness didn't know where to shop."

— ANONYMOUS

There are many powerful emotions than can limit us from having an abundance mentality. They include fear, doubt, and guilt.

In this meditation you can issue your own declaration of independence and feel a newfound freedom.

Mx

Breathe in a sense of freshness and freedom. Exhale, feeling any bindings or ties to old limitations detach and release. Let each breath help you to remember the part of you that is free.

Declare that this truth is self-evident. The declaration "I am now free of old limitations" is a powerful affirmation in itself.

Treasure Chest

"The Best Things in Life Are Free"
— SONG TITLE BY LEW BROWN/BUDDY DeSYLVA

We all have the capacity for receiving and giving unconditional, abundant love. Tap into your internal treasure chest—your heart—with this give-and-take meditation.

> **Mx**
>
> Focus your awareness in the center of your heart and visualize a treasure chest there. Open the lid and see yourself as already having all the whealth you desire and sharing it with others.

The more treasure you remove, the fuller the chest becomes.

Going Up!

"A man with a new idea is a crank until the idea succeeds."

— MARK TWAIN

This meditation is a simple lift to remind you that your fortunes *will* rise. Use it to take you to the next level whenever you feel stuck or stagnant.

> **Mx**
>
> Enter an old-fashioned, elaborate elevator that has an attendant who asks you where you're going. Tell him or her that your intention is to go up!

Another useful affirmation is "I am now moving forward."

Prosperity Tree

"Money is always there, but the pockets change."

—Gertrude Stein

If you've been told that money doesn't grow on trees, this meditation will give you a chance to turn a new leaf on life.

> **Mx**
>
> Imagine planting the seeds of abundance inside yourself. As your sapling grows, take a minute to ask what it needs to continue to grow and bear fruit. See your prosperity tree grow and flourish as each day you check in on its growth.

Prosperity starts within you. Cultivate it!

In-vestments

"I base my fashion taste on what doesn't itch."
—GILDA RADNER

To be "vested" in something means to be fully endowed with power, authority, or rank. A "vestment" is also a garment or ceremonial robe. If your mental chatter is invested in criticizing and belittling yourself, it will drain your prosperity and leave you threadbare. Here is a get-rich scheme to help you become healthy, whealthy, and wise.

> **Mx**
>
> Breathe deeply and picture yourself being covered, surrounded, enveloped, and cloaked with self-assurance. Give your vestments color and texture. In-vest your awareness and thoughts in abundance.

You are your own best in-vestment!

Summary

Finding your own level of prosperity is an internal question that only you can answer. But count on this: if your balance sheet is calculated using an abundance mentality, your personal net worth will reach new highs.

Afterword

The end or the beginning?

At this point, we think you'll agree that the hardest part of meditating is remembering to do it. The uses and benefits of meditation are infinite, and we encourage you to incorporate meditation into your daily routines.

In this book we've included meditations that can be done in the shower; while eating; while going to and from work; in an elevator; while walking, running, or standing still; and while sitting on a chair or lying in bed, so there's no valid excuse for not meditating! You can now meditate *anywhere*, *anytime*.

A Closing Note from Michael

When I first started meditating, I found it a frustrating experience. *I couldn't get it right. It was too much work. I didn't have the time.* I used all the excuses that many of us use when encountering a self-improvement project that might be good for us but we really do not want to do. Dieting, exercise, stopping smoking all elicit similar rationales for noncompletion in one given program or another. We go kicking and screaming until we either find the key to success or we give up!

One day I found myself in a high-stress family situation and "remembered" to use a one-minute centering meditation that I had learned. The results were profound, and I became the master of the situation instead of allowing the situation to master me. I was able to put to use what I had learned in a very practical situation.

I have a favorite line from a poem by Rudyard Kipling titled "If" that runs through my mind often and is a reminder for me to meditate: "If you can keep your head while all about you others are losing theirs and blaming it on you, . . . you'll be a man, my son!"

This was my beginning. I hope that this book can help you to find yours.

A Closing Note from Nancy

All you need to do to re-member and re-mind yourself into wholeness and balance is to *remember* to meditate. I use all sorts of props: affirmations and notes posted at my desk, in the kitchen, bathroom, and throughout the house. There's even a note to myself dangling from the car's rearview mirror:

C
E
N
T
E
R

Another of my reminder notes is *Teach by setting an example*. While meditating for just a minute a day may seem inconsequential, I believe it has profound potential for changing the world one person and one minute at a time.

If each of us takes a minute a day to breathe deeply and connect with the place of center and wholeness within ourselves, and then radiates that example outward to our children, coworkers, family, and friends, we will be teaching a very profound lesson. It only takes a minute!

From Both of Us

The end or the beginning? It's up to you.

We hope you utilize these one-minute meditations to bring a sense of sanity into your busy life. Whether you continue to use these simple, quick meditations, or use them as a stepping-off place to explore more in-depth meditation practices, we wish you well.

If you have a question that we haven't addressed, you may E-mail it to us at medex101@aol.com, and we'll do our best to answer you or point you in the direction of an appropriate resource. You may also learn more about our *Mx* Online Meditation Service and visit the chat room at our website www.meditationexpress.com. You may also inquire about our corporate seminars, public appearances, and upcoming events through the website.

We'd like very much to hear your stories about how you've utilized the meditations in this book and how they've affected your life. Or, if you've made a variation on one of the meditations to better suit you, please let us know, and we may include your story in our next book.

Our mailing address is:

The Meditation Express
P.O. Box 1344
Key West, FL 33041-1344

If these meditations have given you a minute of peace, we can say aaah. We're looking forward to hearing from you.

Appendix A

Questions and Plausible Answers

"It is better to know some of the questions than all of the answers."

—James Thurber

Here we've answered the questions we are most frequently asked about meditating.

Q. Do I need to find a guru if I want to continue to meditate?

A. No. If you would like to be instructed in a particular belief system, such as Buddhism, you may want to seek a teacher, or guru, but you don't have to in order to meditate. If asked who her guru is, Nancy usually quips that her guru is baba ganoush, which is an eggplant salad, but it sounds good. (The term *baba* is a title of respect meaning father, or sire, and Nancy's intent is not to use it disrespectfully.)

Q. Sometimes I start to fall asleep when I meditate. What does this mean?

A. This is a common occurrence, and it simply means that you need to get more sleep. It has nothing to do with your ability to meditate.

Q. My center line changes colors, sometimes it's even black. Should I be worried? I thought my center line should be a light color.

A. Remember, there are no "shoulds" when you're meditating, and you can relax about seeing a black center line. Black usually signifies a transformation and is not something to be afraid of.

You may also think of it as the enriching, deep, refreshing darkness of a night sky.

Q. When should I expect to see the results from meditating?

A. Immediately. Very often, though, the changes in you can be very subtle. It may happen that your friends and coworkers notice that something is different about you before you do.

Q. Are there any times that I shouldn't meditate?

A. Yes, when you're driving or doing something else that requires your full attention. Otherwise, unless you've been told by a medical professional that you have a condition (epilepsy, for instance) that affects your brainwave activity, it's safe to meditate. Meditation works beneficially in conjunction with any medical modality, and many people meditate before surgery or while receiving chemotherapy.

Q. I can't do every meditation in the book. What should I do?

A. Do the meditations that work best for you.

Q. I'm not sure if what I'm doing is really meditating. How will I know when I can *really* meditate?

A. Meditating is like sailing: the act of calming and focusing your thoughts, or being on the water and enjoying the scenery, is what's beneficial. There may be additional benefits: a healthier body, less anger, or more productivity, but it's not a destination to be arrived *at* (that's called *arriving*). You'll have some days when it's easier than others, but trust yourself that you *already know how to meditate*.

Q. My mind keeps wandering. What's wrong?

A. Nothing! Your mind's job is to be active. Your job in meditation is simply to bring it back into focus.

Q. I can't meditate every day. Is it okay if I only meditate a few times a week?

A. Of course. What usually happens, though, is that you'll eventually *want* to meditate as often as possible because you'll start noticing that the days you do meditate seem to "flow." *Any* time you can meditate is a wonderful gift to yourself.

Q. Do I have to believe in a deity to meditate?

A. Meditating helps you to find your own truths. You don't need to be religious for meditation to help you.

Q. Isn't meditation a form of mind control?

A. Perhaps, but the control is coming from inside of *you*, not an outside manipulator. Meditation is about discovering your own truths, remember?

Q. I meditate every day but still get angry or sad or frustrated. Why is this still happening?

A. Meditation isn't a magic pill that gives you a perfect life or even spares you from life's experiences. Meditating *will* give you a stable inner sense of balance in your crazy, hectic life.

Q. Why do some people light incense and candles when they meditate?

A. Some meditators wear special clothes and beads, light candles and incense, or have a special room where they meditate because these things help them to focus or may have a particular significance to them. While enjoyable, none of them are necessary for a beneficial meditation practice.

Q. How can I introduce meditation to my children?

A. Make it fun for them. You can have them count their steps while they're walking or focus on their breathing while you're waiting for something. Make a game out of it. You can easily adapt many of the meditations in this book to fit a child's interests.

P.S. When Nancy teaches meditation to kids, she doesn't use the term *meditation* but calls it Focus Pocus.

Appendix B

Variations on a Theme

"If you lived here, you'd be OM now."

— BUMPER STICKER

The following glossary will help you to explore other practices that you may have heard about or seen advertised. In our attempt to keep things simple and to the point, the descriptions are brief. There is much depth and beauty to all of the following, and we encourage you to explore all that attract you. Where we know of a national organization, we have listed it. Please note that the inclusion—or exclusion—of a modality is not an endorsement or rejection of any particular practice.

Affirmations

Affirmations are positive statements that become part of your subconscious mind through the act of repetition. They can help you to achieve a desired effect or exert an influence in making changes in your life. Phrasing of an affirmation should be in a positive, present tense to set the tone for your desired effect. Please refer to Chapter 12.

Aikido (ah-KEY-doe)

Translated from the Japanese, Aikido means "The Way of Harmony of the Spirit." It is a martial art that places an emphasis not only on motion and dynamics of motion but also on the moral and spiritual aspects of harmony and peace.

Aromatherapy

This ancient healing art makes "scents." In aromatherapy, it is believed that the inhaled scent of an essential oil is conveyed via the olfactory nerve to areas of the brain that can influence emotions and hormonal responses for therapeutic results. In addition, when used in a bath or directly applied to the skin, the plant-based oil is absorbed and carried by body fluids to heal and support the nervous and muscular systems. Several pure essential oils may be blended (in incense, candles, soaps) for harmonious fragrances and effects.

Centering

Centering is a process of finding your own inner state of balance. Just as potters "center" a lump of clay before forming it, you, too, can center yourself. It's a simple way to balance your mind, body, spirit, and emotions for optimum health and wellness, and also to stay centered between the past and the future—in the present moment. Please refer to Chapter 3.

Chanting

Chanting is a mental and physical discipline that encompasses proper articulation of words or phrases, breath control, and attention to posture. In simple terms, "it ain't just singing." Gregorian chants are early Christian practices of this method that have been recorded in recent years and popularly accepted.

Creative Visualization/Guided Imagery

Creative visualization, or guided imagery, is a way of using your mind's eye (your imagination) to create a mental image of what you want in your life. It's a form of conscious and directed daydreaming that many athletes, actors, musicians, and politicians use as part of a successful training program.

Feng Shui (fung SHWAY)

If you have certain areas in your house or office that you prefer over others, it's probably because the colors, shapes, and placements of furniture are in balance. Feng shui is a functional design art that believes that your state of mind and energy affect your environment, and vice versa. Derived from ancient Taoist tradition, it incorporates two Chinese astrological systems and has an elaborate system of rules and principles. In a nutshell, it keeps the energy of an area flowing and healthy. Feng shui consultants can help you design your home or office to support your health, relationships, career, and other aspects of your life.

Global Meditation

Global meditation links thousands of individuals around the world in meditation. Individuals and groups meditate to heal the planet and transform the world with vibrations of love and peace, to expand global consciousness, and to commune with others of similar intent.

Group Meditation

Very often, individuals find it easier to meditate in the presence of other meditators. They claim it is easier to stay focused and to go deeper into focusing within themselves. Group meditation may also include guided meditation, where an experienced meditator will verbally lead or guide the intention and direction of the meditation.

Guided Meditation

A guided meditation leads, instructs, and assists the meditator in achieving a specific outcome, such as relaxation, healing, or expanded awareness. Guided meditations can be anywhere from 10 minutes to an hour in length.

Hypnotherapy

Hypnotherapy is a therapeutic process that has become widely accepted and clinically proven to help in the management of many medical and psychological situations such as stress, anxiety, phobias, substance abuse, eating disorders, pain management, and so on. In hypnosis, an induction to an altered state of consciousness takes place. This activates the relaxation response and accesses the subconscious, thus enabling the mind to become suggestible to change. For more information, contact the National Guild of Hypnotists, Inc., P.O. Box 308, Merrimack, NH 03054-0308, (603) 429-9438.

Self-hypnosis is similar to hypnosis, varying in that the induction and therapeutic work is done by oneself, upon oneself.

Neuro-Linguistic Programming (NLP) is a form of hypnotic technique created in 1975 by Richard Bandler and John Grindler. It uses the method of *modeling* as a motivational approach in improving interpersonal skills, bettering personal performance, and accessing other tools for personal development. NLP claims to utilize hypnotic techniques for helping to achieve personal change quickly and without formal induction.

Mandala

A mandala is a meditative art form that expresses a mantra in a written or drawn form. It is usually given to the meditator by a teacher, or guru (see *mantra*).

Mantra

In the traditional sense, a mantra is a sound, word, or phrase that is given to a meditator by a spiritual teacher. A universal mantra is *Aum*, believed to represent the primal sound from which all things came into being, and its derivatives *Om* or *Amen*. The mantra is focused upon and repeated in meditation, in the belief that the sound or word(s) has a special energy or awareness and invokes a special power within one's self. Mantras may be repeated silently, verbally, sung solo or in a group (see *chanting*). They may also be written or drawn (see *mandala*).

Meditation

Meditation takes many shapes and forms. Some are easy, some are not. Some are physical, some are spiritual. Many types of meditation attempt to have you clear your mind of all thoughts and seek a calm, quiet place within yourself as a sanctuary. Other types of meditation attempt to have you focus on a single point, thought, or object. There are many variations on these themes. The one thing that they all have in common is the universal thread that in order for you to benefit from meditation, you have to remember to do it!

Mindfulness Meditation

This type of meditation practice asks you first to pay attention to a single focus to allow yourself to find a place of calmness and serenity, and then to allow this focal point to expand to include any other observations that might enter your field of consciousness. You are asked not to weigh or analyze the content of your attention but just to observe it nonjudgmentally.

Psychoneuroimmunology (PNI)

PNI is a scientific discipline that studies and validates that you are what you think. Your mental and emotional states are transmitted into your immune and nervous systems (via chemical secretions into the bloodstream and cerebrospinal fluid). PNI has shown how your thoughts and feelings can determine your health and lends credence to the merits of meditation, positive thinking, creative visualization, and medical uses of laughter as a healing aid.

Qi Gong (chee GONG)

Translated literally, Qi Gong means "Energy Cultivation." It is a grouping of physical exercises that is deeply rooted in ancient Chinese history. The exercises offer the intention of benefiting your energy or "chi" and can increase your longevity as well as your sense of harmony with yourself and the world.

Siddha Yoga Meditation

Open to everyone of all faiths and nationalities, with more than 600 centers worldwide, Siddha Yoga meditation is rooted in the wisdom of India's ancient sages. Its present leader, Swami Chidvilasananda, affectionately known as Gurumayi, is a Siddha Guru. She is acknowledged to have the power to give others the inner experience of God through a spiritual awakening. The practice of Siddha Yoga meditation enables seekers to live with an ever-increasing sense of their inner divinity. For more information: SYDA Foundation, P.O. Box 600, South Fallsburg, NY 12779-0600, (845) 434-2000 ext. 2202.

T'ai Chi (tie CHEE)

In China it is not uncommon to see large groups of a hundred or more people practicing T'ai Chi in public parks. T'ai Chi is an ancient Chinese martial art practice that is now popular throughout the world as both a fighting art and a healing art. It is considered one of the exercise categories under Qi Gong. It consists generally of 108 individual movements that are connected together in a universal order. Forms of T'ai Chi have been developed that have fewer movements and can be used by beginners or people too ill to complete the longer form.

Toning

Toning is the practice of sounding elongated vowels on the premise that self-generated sound is a vibration that resonates throughout your body and draws your awareness inward. The seven vowel sounds are each vocalized on a long exhale at a pitch that is comfortable for the individual. Toning promotes deep breathing and long exhalations and often releases tension, promotes relaxation, or energizes the practitioner. Toning may be done alone or in a group, while seated or during movement, such as yoga.

Transcendental Meditation (TM)

Led by Maharishi Mahesh Yogi, TM is practiced by over five million people of all faiths worldwide. It was first introduced to Western awareness by The Beatles in the late 1960s. Since then, TM has been scientifically validated by numerous studies at independent research institutions in 30 countries to reduce stress and improve health, increase vitality, and even reduce crime. TM relaxes a practitioner's physical body and calms the mind so that it is able to transcend mental activity and thus experience a state of restful alertness called Transcendental Consciousness. For more information: 888-LEARN TM (532-7686).

Yoga

When most people think of yoga, they think of the image of people turning themselves into physical pretzels. In actuality, the term *yoga* means to unite or make whole—the joining of the human soul with the Universal Soul. Today, yoga in its many forms has been embraced by millions of people of all faiths. There are as many schools of yoga as there are schools of fish. What follows are what are considered to be the Four Main Paths of Yoga, which embody the many schools.

Bhakti Yoga is the path of Devotion or Divine Love. It is considered to be heart based and is a path of devotional service to the divine, a great task, or one's guru.

Jnana Yoga is the Yoga of Knowledge or Wisdom. This is an intellectual form of yoga for practitioners who contemplate philosophical ideas in their search for truth.

Karma Yoga is the Yoga of Action. Karma means "to do" and refers to the principle of cause and effect. Practitioners believe that through meditation and by surrendering all personal motives for selfish desire they will change their thoughts and feelings to enact *causes* that will result in beneficial *effects* for fulfillment.

Raja Yoga is the Science of Physical and Mental Control. It includes the school of Hatha yoga and is the practice most Westerners think of when they see the word *yoga*. It is physical yoga that conditions the body so that the mind can practice meditation without obstacles. The yoga positions are comfortable, stable postures that strengthen and increase flexibility in the body through breath work and stretching. These yoga practices can be relaxing, invigorating, and even aerobic. The benefits include increased circulation, improved immune function, spinal health, and stress reduction. Many people further pursue Hatha yoga practices as a way to develop their spiritual awakening, as well.

Zen Meditation

Zen meditation is closely associated with Zen Buddhism. It is primarily a seated meditation with various set "positions" or postures that are essential to the ultimate goal of Zen meditation, which is the study of the self and, ultimately, enlightenment. Clearing the mind and attaining a peaceful state is another goal of Zen meditation.

Appendix C

*Some Suggestions for Further Reading
and Listening*

"*You ain't heard nothin' yet, folks.*"
—AL JOLSON IN *THE JAZZ SINGER*

*Spiritual Abundance: Meditations and Affirmations on
    Prosperity for Every Day of the Year* by David Stuart
    Alexander. Putnam Publishing Group, 1997.

The Relaxation Response by Herbert Benson, M.D.
    Morrow and Company, 1975.

Minding the Body, Mending the Mind by Joan Borysenko, Ph.D. Bantam Books, 1987.

Journey of Awakening by Ram Dass. Bantam Books, 1978.

Meditations for Manifesting: Morning and Evening Meditations to Literally Create Your Heart's Desire by Wayne Dyer. Hay House (audio), 1995.

Creative Visualization: Use the Power of Your Imagination to Create What You Want in Your Life by Shakti Gawain. New World Library, 1995.

Living in the Light: A Guide to Personal and Planetary Transformation by Shakti Gawain. Bantam Books, 1993.

The Miracle of Mindfulness: A Manual on Meditation by Thich Nhat Hanh. Beacon Press, 1976.

The Healer Within by Roger Jahnke. HarperSanFrancisco, 1997.

How to Meditate by Lawrence LeShan, Ph.D. Bantam Books (reissue), 1984.

Meditating to Attain a Healthy Body Weight by Lawrence LeShan, Ph.D. Doubleday, 1994.

Money Meditations for Women: Thoughts, Exercises, Resources, and Affirmations for Creating Prosperity by Jo Ann Lordahl, Ph.D. Celestial Arts, 1994.

Dr. Dean Ornish's Program for Reversing Heart Disease by Dr. Dean Ornish. Ballantine Books, 1990.

Meditations for Finding the Key to Good Health: Open the Door to a Healthier You by Bernie Siegel, M.D. Hay House (audio), 1992.

Mindfulness Meditation: Cultivating the Wisdom of Your Body and Mind by Jon Kabat-Zinn. Simon & Schuster (audio), 1995.

Wherever You Go, There You Are: Mindfulness Meditation in Everyday Life by Jon Kabat-Zinn. Hyperion, 1995.

Index